I0428412

Everything Dr. Msimang Knows About The South African Health Crisis

Knowl Itall

Knowl Itall

www.ingramcontent.com/pod-product-compliance
Lightning Source LLC
Chambersburg PA
CBHW070550290526
45790CB00002B/623
* 9 7 8 1 5 0 2 5 8 6 7 0 4 *